COUNTDOWN TO EXTINCTION

ANIMALS IN DANGER!

DAVID BURNIE

OXFORD

UNIVERSITY PRESS

OXFORD
UNIVERSITY PRESS

Great Clarendon Street, Oxford OX2 6DP

Oxford University Press is a department of the University of Oxford.
It furthers the University's objective of excellence in research,
scholarship, and education by publishing worldwide in

Oxford   New York

Auckland   Cape Town   Dar es Salaam   Hong Kong   Karachi
Kuala Lumpur   Madrid   Melbourne   Mexico City   Nairobi
New Delhi   Shanghai   Taipei   Toronto

With offices in

Argentina   Austria   Brazil   Chile   Czech Republic   France   Greece
Guatemala   Hungary   Italy   Japan   Poland   Portugal   Singapore
South Korea   Switzerland   Thailand   Turkey   Ukraine   Vietnam

Oxford is a registered trade mark of Oxford University Press
in the UK and in certain other countries

British Library Cataloguing in Publication Data

Data available

ISBN: 978-0-19-911600-3

10 9 8 7 6 5 4 3 2 1

Originated by Oxford University Press
Created by Toucan Books Ltd

Printed in Thailand by Imago

Contents

Introduction

Roughly every 15 minutes, somewhere in the world, an animal becomes extinct. You won't hear about it when it happens, and you're very unlikely to see it reported on TV. But the extinction clock keeps ticking, 24 hours a day. Every year, more than 30,000 kinds of animal disappear. It's a frightening figure, and it is growing bigger all the time.

Extinction is not something new. In fact, it has been taking place since life began on Earth, more than three billion years ago. It's part of the way nature works: new species gradually evolve, replacing older ones that are less good at survival. But in today's world, extinction is happening thousands of times faster than ever before, and huge numbers of species are now on the danger list. These include more than 500 kinds of mammals,

Every year, MORE THAN 30,000 kinds of *animals* DISAPPEAR.

about the same number of birds, and more than 1,000 different amphibians. Unless something is done to help these animals, it will soon be their turn to disappear.

The last time anything like this occurred was 65 million years ago. A giant meteorite hit the Earth, creating a worldwide disaster that killed off the dinosaurs. This time, the extinctions are being caused by us, and the way that we live. We cannot stop the clock, but we can slow it down. It's vital that we do, because once an animal becomes extinct, nothing can be done to bring it back.

DAVID BURNIE

In the Hunters' Sights

THOUSANDS OF YEARS AGO, people relied on hunting to survive. Today, almost all of our food comes from farms, but hunting still goes on. In most countries, it is strictly regulated, but illegal hunters – or poachers – ignore the law, and kill hundreds of thousands of animals every year. People hunt animals for food, for money, or simply for the thrill of making a kill. Poaching is a worldwide problem, and it has pushed some animals to the brink of extinction.

With their huge ears and sensitive trunks, African elephants are good at hearing or smelling signs of danger. But keen senses are not enough to protect them from hunters armed with guns.

Prehistoric extinctions

THE FIRST HUMANS LIVED in Africa, more than 200,000 years ago. From here, they spread across the world. Compared to their prey, they were crafty and cunning. By using weapons and working together, they managed to kill animals far bigger than themselves. Some of these animals were already in trouble, because the world's climate was changing. Human hunters made life harder still, wiping out the stragglers that managed to survive.

END OF THE MASTODON

The American mastodon died out about 10,000 years ago, when the last Ice Age was coming to an end. This elephant-like mammal stood three metres high, making it a tempting target for human hunters. In some parts of North America, researchers have found stone spear tips among mastodon bones – evidence that the first Americans ate mastodon meat.

In Europe, prehistoric cave paintings show animals that people once hunted. They include reindeer, horses, bison, and the aurochs – a wild ox with long, sharply pointed horns, which became extinct in the early 1600s.

CAVE PAINTINGS

are *windows on the past,* bringing extinct animals back to life.

BACK FROM THE *brink*

Long ago, the European bison (or wisent) roamed across most of Europe. However, it was hunted for many centuries, and the last wild bison was killed in the early 1900s. Fortunately, some bison survived in zoos, and in the 1950s, the species was reintroduced into the wild. Today, there are about 3,000 European bison. One of the biggest herds is in the Białowieza Forest, in eastern Poland.

Giant Kangaroo   *Giant Wombat*   *Giant Goanna*

EXTINCT AUSTRALIANS

At one time, Australia was home to many outsize animals, but all of these giant species vanished soon after people reached Australia, more than 40,000 years ago.

GIANT JAWS

This fossilized jaw bone belonged to a giant kangaroo. Unlike today's kangaroos, it had back feet with a single hoof, and probably used its front paws to pull leafy branches towards its mouth.

As dead as a dodo

IMAGINE HAVING A PAIR of wings but not being able to fly. It sounds strange, but it makes perfect sense if you are a bird that feeds on the ground. For the dodo, being flightless was not a problem – until human hunters arrived in its remote island home of Mauritius in 1638. Almost as soon as people stepped ashore, the slaughter began.

TOO TAME TO MISS

The dodo was a giant member of the pigeon family, with a thickset body and tiny wings. It lived in dense forest, nested on the ground, and fed on fallen fruit. Like many animals from remote islands, it had no fear of humans, which made it very easy to kill.

ARABIAN OSTRICH

Today, wild ostriches are found only in Africa, but until recent times, ostriches also lived in Arabia and other parts of the Middle East. As this painting from an old manuscript shows, Arabian ostriches looked very much like African ones, although they were smaller. For centuries, these birds were hunted with bows and arrows, but they were killed off when hunters started using guns.

In just 50 years, the dodo was wiped out, but hunters were not solely to blame. With people came pigs, dogs and cats, which destroyed the dodos' nests and ate their eggs and chicks.

spotlight on giant birds

The elephant bird, which lived on the island of Madagascar, weighed nearly half a tonne. It had tiny wings, but a kick that could kill. Human hunters finished it off in the late 1500s.

EXTINCTION AT SEA

On 3 July 1844, two bird-hunters from Iceland killed a male and female great auk. Although the hunters did not know it, this was the moment when the great auk became extinct. Great auks looked very much like penguins, but they lived in the North Atlantic instead of the southern hemisphere.

HEADS UP

Standing nearly two metres tall, these ostriches are on the alert for any sign of trouble. Ostriches are off the danger list, but in the past, they were hunted all over Africa, for their feathers as well as for their meat. Many other birds – from egrets to albatrosses – have been massacred by feather-hunters, and some are now close to extinction.

Food on the hoof

Buffalo – or bison – once lived in huge herds on America's Great Plains. Native Americans killed them only so that they had enough to eat, but in the 1800s, Europeans started to hunt with guns. Hundreds of thousands of buffaloes were killed, shot at from horseback and from trains, sometimes just for fun. Fortunately, the buffalo did not die out, but it came dangerously close.

END OF THE LINE
This photograph, taken during the late 1800s, shows piles of buffalo bones waiting to be loaded onto a train. Buffalo bones were ground up to make fertilizer, while buffalo hides were used to make clothes and shoes. At one time, there were 50 million buffalo, but by 1900, only a few thousand were left on the Great Plains. Today, there are about 200,000, most of which live in national parks.

LUCKY BREAK

Mountain zebras, from South Africa, are much rarer than the zebras that live on Africa's grassy plains. One kind – the Cape mountain zebra – is protected by its own national park. During the 1950s, the park had fewer than 10 zebras. Today, there are more than 200, and new herds have been started in places where these animals used to live.

In the last 250 years, more than 20 kinds of hoofed mammal have been hunted into extinction, or have come close to it. Species on the danger list include the Arabian oryx, several species of gazelle, and an Asian antelope called the saiga.

BACK FROM THE *brink*

Przewalski's horses, from Mongolia, are the only truly wild horses left on Earth. In Mongolia, they were hunted to extinction by the 1960s, but in 1992, a new herd was formed, made of animals that had been bred in zoos. Small and tough, these horses can cope with hot dry summers and bitter winter cold.

Hunters *target* the ARABIAN ORYX for its spectacular horns.

PRICE ON ITS HEAD

For centuries, the horns of the Arabian oryx were prized by collectors, and by the 1970s, the species had disappeared from the wild. It was saved by a special breeding programme, but this beautiful oryx still faces a struggle to survive.

shot from the skies

UNTIL THE 1800S, American passenger pigeons were the commonest birds in the world. A single flock could contain more than a billion birds, so hitting them was child's play, and hunters often shot millions when a flock was on the move. But the carnage could not last. The flocks shrank rapidly, and by 1914, the passenger pigeon had become extinct.

THE LAST SURVIVOR

These are the stuffed remains of George, the last male passenger pigeon, who died in captivity in 1910. George's mate, Martha, survived for another four years, and died at the age of 29. Martha had spent her whole life in a zoo. Once George had gone, she never saw another passenger pigeon again.

spotlight on pigeons and doves

There are nearly 300 kinds of pigeons and doves. Some are common, but 26 are endangered, and 11 of these are threatened with extinction. Many of these species feed on fruit and live in tropical forests.

DANGEROUS VOYAGE

In spring, flocks of turtle doves migrate from North Africa to Europe, to nest and raise their young. As the birds fly through narrow mountain passes and across islands, hunters lie in wait, shooting them as they fly past. Every year, thousands of turtle doves are shot from the skies before they have a chance to breed.

CROWNING GLORY

The Victoria crowned pigeon is one of the world's biggest and most spectacular pigeons, with a chicken-sized body and a beautiful lacy crest. It lives in the forests of New Guinea, where it feeds on the ground. These pigeons can fly, but it takes them time to get into the air, and so it is easy for hunters and their dogs to kill them. To make life tougher still, their forest home is shrinking fast.

ONE FLOCK of *passenger pigeons* was estimated to contain 2,230,272,000 birds.

BACK FROM THE *brink*

The pink pigeon, from the island of Mauritius, is one of the great success stories of animal conservation. During the 1990s, its numbers fell to just ten, but conservationists acted in time, catching some of the pigeons and sending them to zoos. The birds did well in captivity, and many of their young have been released back into the wild.

Tusk trouble

SOME OF THE WORLD'S biggest land mammals face danger from hunters. Elephants are hunted for their ivory tusks, and rhinos for their horns. Ivory is used for carved ornaments, while ground-up rhino horn is used in traditional Eastern medicine. It is against the law to sell ivory or rhino horns, but these illegal goods fetch colossal prices, so poaching is very difficult to stop.

BEACON OF HOPE

Between 1973 and 1989, nearly 90 per cent of Kenya's elephants were killed by poachers. In 1989, the president of Kenya set fire to more than 2,000 confiscated tusks to show that Kenya's wildlife service was determined to crack down on the illegal ivory trade. Since then, Kenya's elephants have started to recover, but poachers still pose a threat.

On the
BLACK MARKET,
a *single tusk*
can be worth MORE THAN
£10,000.

spotlight on elephants......

There are about 600,000 elephants in Africa, but only about 50,000 elephants in Asia. The Asian elephant is officially classified as endangered, while the African elephant is vulnerable, meaning it could become endangered.

SECURITY PATROL

Rhinos are at the top of the target list for poachers, and the African black rhino has been particularly badly hit. Today, armed wardens watch over many rhinos, keeping poachers at bay. Rhinos have even been fitted with radio transmitters, hidden inside their horns, to make it easier for wardens to track them.

UNEASY RIDE

For thousands of years, Asian elephants have been tamed and put to work. They have smaller tusks than African elephants, so are at less risk from poachers, but they are still in danger. The main problem is that their natural habitat – tropical forest – is disappearing fast. Every year, it becomes harder for wild elephants to find enough food.

Vanishing cats

OF ALL THE WORLD'S big predators, tigers face the greatest struggle for survival in the wild. A century ago, there were more than 100,000 tigers in existence. Today, there are fewer than 5,000, and several hundred are killed every year. To make matters worse still, tigers need lots of space, and on a planet crowded with people, that's getting very hard to find.

MAKING A KILLING

These skins come from tigers that were illegally killed in the wild. For poachers, a dead tiger can mean big money. As well as selling the tiger's skin, poachers can trade the bones and other body parts for use in Chinese medicines. However, the biggest profits are often made by the illegal traders who deal in tiger remains.

Big cats have long been hunted for their fur, but the world's biggest cat – the tiger – faces many other threats as well. Many experts think it is only a matter of time before this magnificent animal becomes extinct in the wild.

BACK INTO THE WILD

With a single bound, an Amur (or Siberian) tiger jumps for freedom after being rescued from a snare. Amur tigers, which live in the far east of Russia, are the world's biggest cats, but they face constant danger from poachers, who hunt them for their skins and their bones.

BACK FROM THE *brink*

One of the world's rarest cats lives on Iriomote-jima, a small subtropical island in the south of Japan. The Iriomote cat, which is about the same size as a pet cat, lives in dense forest and was not discovered until 1967. Only about 100 of these cats are left in the wild, but they are carefully protected. Road signs on Iriomote-jima warn motorists to watch out for them.

TOP CAT

The snow leopard lives in the grassland and mountains of Central Asia, hunting at altitudes of up to 6,000 metres. Its beautiful coat keeps it warm, and it wraps its long tail around itself like a scarf when it curls up on the ground. Hunters target these cats for their fur, but farmers also persecute them, because they sometimes feed on cattle and sheep.

The wildlife trade

EVERY YEAR, CUSTOMS OFFICIALS uncover hundreds of thousands of animals hidden aboard trucks, ships and planes. Most of these forced travellers are caught in the wild, and then packed up without food, water, or even enough space to move. The wildlife trade is cruel, and it's also harmful, because it can drive rare species towards extinction.

Smuggled birds OFTEN DIE *before they reach* their destination.

Illegal animal traders earn millions of dollars every year. As well as smuggling wildlife, some sell the animals and their products through the internet. Because the internet works worldwide, this kind of trading is very hard to stamp out.

TORTOISES IN TRANSIT

These baby star tortoises were found in a passenger's hand luggage in Singapore. Star tortoises are a favourite with animal smugglers because their attractive shells ensure that they fetch a good price. This suitcase contained nearly 500 tortoises, valued at up to £8,000.

FLYING FREE

Queen Alexandra's birdwing is the world's largest butterfly, and a favourite target for illegal collectors. It lives in New Guinea and is already endangered by deforestation. Tropical beetles are also popular with smugglers.

GOING, going, GONE!

SHELL SHOCK

Shells are popular souvenirs, but buying them can endanger wildlife because they are often collected from living animals. The shell trade harms many molluscs that live on coral reefs, and also the nautilus (above), which has a beautiful spiral shell.

BORDER GUARD

Since 1975, an international agreement, called CITES, has helped to prevent unsustainable trade in wildlife. CITES stands for the Convention on International Trade in Endangered Species of Wild Fauna and Flora.

Vanishing Habitats

THE WORLD WE LIVE IN is changing faster than ever before. Thanks to humans, all kinds of habitats are being damaged or even destroyed. When a habitat disappears, its wildlife disappears, too. Tropical forests top the list of habitats under threat. Every year, huge areas are cut down for timber, and to make way for farms. The soil is poor, and farming it is hard, but for people who have no land, it is better than nothing at all. In many other habitats, from wetlands to coral reefs, the basic problem is the same.

Cracked mud and tree stumps are all that remain of this forest in Thailand. The forest was once home to many different mammals, birds and insects, but all of them have disappeared.

shrinking forests

TROPICAL FORESTS ARE THE world's fastest shrinking habitats. All around the globe – from South America to Southeast Asia – they are being felled to produce timber and to clear land for farms. These forests are home to thousands of different kinds of animals. Some are widespread, but many are found in only one place in the world.

NIGHT PATROL

The aye-aye lives in Madagascar – an island that has lost half its forest cover in the last 50 years. It comes out to feed at night, using its bony fingers to find grubs living under bark. Ayes-ayes have never been common, but they are now edging close to extinction. Like many other animals on the island, the aye-aye's only home is Madagascar.

RAREST RHINO

The Javan rhino used to be found in forests throughout Southeast Asia. Today, it is one of the world's rarest forest mammals – experts think that less than 100 still survive. Most of them live in a small part of the island of Java, with just a small number more in Vietnam. Javan rhinos are shy and secretive, so these few survivors are seldom seen.

SNAPPED

A Sumatran rabbit takes its own photo by triggering an automatic camera. For 25 years, this forest rabbit was thought to be extinct, until one hopped past a camera in 1997. Automatic cameras can be left in the forest for weeks, and can even take pictures after dark – a time when endangered animals are often most active.

SNAKE ON THE MOVE

Snakes are not everyone's favourite animals, but they play an important part in the balance of nature. Dumeril's boa, from Madagascar, is one of many snakes that are threatened by deforestation. It kills its prey by squeezing them in its coils, and uses its beautiful camouflage to hide in the dappled shade on the forest floor.

ENDANGERED EAGLES

Tropical forests are home to some of the world's biggest and rarest birds of prey. The harpy eagle, from Central and South America, feeds on sloths and monkeys, snatching them from trees as it flies past. Harpy eagles raise only one chick every two to three years, and they need lots of space – something that is becoming hard for them to find.

Monkeys in trouble

IF YOU DEPEND ON TREES for your survival, forest clearance is the biggest disaster that you could possibly face. That's exactly the problem for most of the world's primates. These animals range from big gorillas and monkeys to squirrel-sized tamarins, and all of them need trees for food, security and shelter.

SECOND CHANCE
These young orang-utans were brought to a rescue centre in Borneo after their mother was killed by hunters. Bewildered by their surroundings, they cling to each other for comfort. With proper care, they have a chance of growing up normally, and will eventually be released back into the wild.

PATCHWORK HOME
Woolly spider monkeys live in Brazil's Atlantic forest - a habitat close to cities on Brazil's eastern coast. Their forest home has been shrinking for centuries, and today less than a tenth of it is left. Most of it is in small patches, making it even harder for the monkeys to survive.

A fifth OF ALL PRIMATES ARE IN serious danger.

DOUBLE TROUBLE

Mountain gorillas face two deadly dangers – forest clearance and a home that has been ravaged by war. These gorillas live in the forests of central Africa, where bands of marauding soldiers shoot wild animals for food. Protecting the gorillas is highly dangerous, and park rangers run a real risk of being killed themselves.

BACK FROM THE *brink*

With its brilliantly coloured fur, the golden lion tamarin is one of the most endangered mammals in South America. It seemed doomed to extinction in the 1970s, but thanks to an international conservation programme, it has been saved. There are now about 1,000 tamarins in the wild, and 500 in captivity.

FAMILY GROUP

Like the aye-aye, ring-tailed lemurs live in Madagascar – an island that is like a primate ark. This single island is home to more than two dozen kinds of primate, and none of them live anywhere else in the world. But in recent decades, Madagascar's forests have been disappearing at a frightening rate, leaving many of these animals in desperate straits.

Predators on the run

IT IS EASY TO ADMIRE big predators, but not so nice to have them on your doorstep. That's why people have hunted bears, wolves and eagles for hundreds of years. Unfortunately, so much land is now used by humans that these natural hunters are running out of the space they need to feed.

MAKING A COMEBACK

Wolves have a scary reputation, but it is extremely rare for them to attack people. They once lived all over North America, Europe and Asia, but now they are common only in the far north. These wolves have been reintroduced into the USA's Yellowstone National Park.

LAST SURVIVOR

This is one of the last photos ever taken of a thylacine – a stripy, dog-shaped marsupial from Australia and Tasmania. Thylacines died out in Australia about 2,000 years ago, but they clung on in Tasmania until the 20th century. Tasmanian farmers shot them to protect their sheep, and the last survivor died in 1936, alone in a zoo.

AERIAL STRIKE

With its two-metre wingspan, the Philippine eagle is one of the world's heaviest and most powerful birds of prey. It lives by snatching monkeys out of the treetops, but it needs a huge hunting territory to get enough food. After years of deforestation, its habitat has shrunk dramatically. With only about 250 eagles left, it's at the top of the critical list.

THE WORLD'S RAREST CAT

Few people ever get to see a Spanish lynx, because it is the most endangered wild cat in the world. It lives in remote woodlands in southern Spain, using its incredibly keen eyesight and hearing to catch rabbits and birds. No one knows exactly how many lynxes are left, but it may be as few as 100 – barely enough to keep the species alive.

BACK FROM THE *brink*

Centuries ago, brown bears were common in mountains across the whole of Europe. Today, after centuries of persecution, they live only in remote places, as far as possible from people. But work is underway to bring the brown bear back. Several have been released in the Pyrenees, in southern France, where the species had completely died out. Not everyone is keen on the plan, however. Sheep farmers fear for their flocks with brown bears on the prowl.

Dwindling wetlands

WETLANDS AREN'T THE EASIEST places to explore, but they are a vital habitat for wild animals, such as otters, fish, and frogs, and about a fifth of the world's birds. Unfortunately, wetlands are in trouble. More than half of them have already been drained, leaving the animals who live there with nowhere to go.

GENTLE GIANTS

Lounging on a riverbank, these South American giant otters look completely relaxed. But things are not as peaceful as they seem. Riverbank forests are being cut down, and boats churn up the water where the otters fish, sometimes hitting them as they speed past. To make matters worse, giant otters are also hunted for their fur.

LAW IN ACTION

Newts lay their eggs in water, and they need ponds to breed. At one time, ponds were common in the countryside, but today they are often filled in. In Britain, the great crested newt was particularly threatened, and the law had to step in to save it. Today, it is illegal to disturb these newts, so their breeding ponds are safe.

HIGH AND DRY

The Aral Sea, in Central Asia, is an example of just how bad things can get when people interfere with wetlands. Actually a giant lake, it has been drying up for decades, because so much of its water is used for farming. It has shrunk to less than half its original size, and many fishing boats have been left stranded far from the shore.

Spotlight on the Devil's Hole pupfish...

The Devil's Hole pupfish has the smallest range of any fish on Earth: a single desert spring in Nevada. The spring has to be carefully monitored, because pollution could wipe out the entire species in hours. At present, there are fewer than 500 of these tiny fish left.

DANGER ON ICE

For sheer elegance, few wetland birds beat Japanese cranes. At one time, they looked set to become extinct in Japan, but they have been saved by protecting the lakes where they gather to perform spectacular courtship dances on the ice.

FAST FOOD

Box turtles have a neat way of getting out of trouble: they pull in their heads and legs, and then shut up their shells using a special hinge. Unfortunately, this does not protect them from the two biggest threats they face – wetland drainage, and people on the lookout for food.

Coral reefs

DIVING IN A CORAL REEF IS one of the most exciting experiences in the world. The corals themselves have extraordinary shapes, and many of the fish are so bright that they look freshly painted. That – at least – is what a healthy reef is like. But tragically, many of the world's reefs are no longer like this. Hit by pollution, over-fishing and climate change, reefs are dying, which means that their animals are vanishing too.

HEALTHY REEF

Coral reefs are built up by tiny animals, and it's easy to tell when they are in good health. They live in groups, forming hard skeletons that look like underwater plants. Living corals are often brightly coloured, and the crevices between them are full of fish, which dart about catching food and steering clear of their enemies.

SHELL COLLECTING

This spotty animal is a cowrie – a kind of sea snail that grazes on coral reefs. Beneath its outer skin is a beautifully shiny shell, with its own rich colours and patterns. Selling tropical seashells has become big business, and in some coral reefs, so many have been collected that they are now becoming rare. Picking up empty shells does no harm, but buying them encourages people to collect yet more shells, killing the animals inside before putting them on sale.

BLEACHED REEF

This reef has been hit by coral bleaching. When the water gets too warm, corals shed the tiny microbes that give them their colour. If the water stays warm, they die and the reef no longer grows. The dead coral starts to break up, and soon very few animals are left. Without urgent help, three-quarters of the world's reefs could be dead by 2050.

REEF REPAIR

Coral reefs can repair themselves, but it's a slow process that takes many years. Recently, scientists have started trying to speed things up by 'planting' pieces of living coral on the sea floor. The pieces of coral are held in place by wire netting or concrete weights. As they grow, they create homes for fish and other animals.

OVER-FRIENDLY FISH

This magnificent humphead wrasse has no fear of humans, and is quite happy to have its skin tickled and stroked. Unfortunately for coral reef fish, being tame can be fatal. That's because spearfishers often stalk coral reefs, and tame fish make easy targets. Local spearfishers usually hunt for food, but tourists often do it just for fun. By killing the biggest and oldest fish, they make it harder for fish to reproduce.

Introduced Species

IF ANIMALS ARE RELEASED in faraway places, they can have a catastrophic effect on local wildlife. The following story illustrates this rule of nature well. In 1935, a plane landed in Australia with some very unusual passengers. On board were 102 cane toads – South American amphibians with big mouths and even bigger appetites. They were brought to Australia to control sugar-cane beetles, but the plan soon came unstuck. In their new home, the toads spread at an incredible rate, devouring all kinds of animals, from small marsupials to baby birds. Today, they are still on the move, threatening even more of Australia's native animals.

Adult cane toads can weigh more than a kilogram, and they eat almost anything that will fit into their mouths. Cane toads and their tadpoles have poisonous skin, so few animals are able to attack them.

Islands apart

BEFORE PEOPLE STARTED TRAVELLING the oceans, remote islands were completely cut off from the rest of the world. Many were home to strange and unique animals, found nowhere else on Earth. But with humans came big changes, as well as wily predators, such as rats and cats. Together, they have pushed island wildlife right to the top of the extinction list.

FEEDING AT FLOWERS

This beautiful male 'i'iwi is feeding on nectar from flowers. The bird is found only in the Hawaiian Islands, and it relies on Hawaiian plants. Unfortunately, the islands have undergone huge changes since the arrival of humans. Pigs and goats have destroyed the vegetation, and mosquitoes have brought in diseases. More than 20 of the 'i'iwi's close relatives have already become extinct.

BACK FROM THE *brink*

During the 1950s, there were only about 30 Hawaiian geese left in the wild. Today, there are more than 1,200, and the number is growing every year. This amazing turnaround came after geese were collected and bred in captivity, then released into the wild.

TRAPPED IN THE TREETOPS

Fiji is the only home of this spectacular, but critically endangered lizard, the Fiji crested iguana. It feeds on leaves and spends its life in trees, but all over Fiji, wandering herds of goats nibble away at young saplings, preventing the forest regrowing. As a result, the iguana's habitat is slowly vanishing, and with it, its chances of survival.

In the last five centuries, hundreds of animals from remote islands have become extinct. One of them – the Stephens Island wren of New Zealand – died out in 1895, just three years after it was discovered.

ReDiscovery

One of the world biggest stick insects – up to 15cm long with a body as thick as a finger – comes from Lord Howe Island, a remote volcanic outcrop in the Pacific Ocean. This rare insect was thought to have died out in 1930, but in 2001, a rock climber spotted it on Ball's Pyramid, an even smaller island nearby.

SLIMY INTRUDERS

Measuring up to 20cm long, the giant African land snail has been introduced into many islands in the Pacific and the Caribbean. It out-eats smaller snails, and has driven many of them into extinction. These giant snails are male and female at the same time, and they sometimes can fertilize their own eggs. As a result, it only takes one to start a snail plague.

GALÁPAGOS GIANT TORTOISES

Monster tortoises once lived in many tropical islands, including Java, Madagascar and the Seychelles. Today, the biggest numbers are in the Galápagos Islands in the Pacific Ocean. Here, they are carefully protected, but they still face serious problems. Wild goats eat their food, which makes it hard for them to grow large enough to breed.

Land of the Moas

THE FIRST HUMAN SETTLERS in New Zealand discovered some of the strangest animals in the world. Instead of mammals, there were giant flightless birds called moas, and insects the size of mice. But people brought huge changes. Today, moas are extinct, and many native animals are fighting for survival.

man   cassowary   ostrich   moa

FAMILY OF GIANTS

New Zealand originally had more than a dozen kinds of moa. The biggest species stood about 3.5m high and would have towered above the ostrich and cassowary – the tallest and heaviest birds today. By about 1500, moas had been hunted to extinction.

LIZARD LOOKALIKE

Tuataras look like lizards, but they belong to an ancient group of reptiles that are midway between lizards and snakes. There are only two species left in the world. Both are endangered, and both live in New Zealand.

TUATARAS *have existed* for more than 200 MILLION years.

Some of New Zealand's most endangered animals have been moved to offshore islands. Here, they are safe from introduced predators, such as stoats and rats, which have ravaged wildlife on the mainland.

...ENDANGERED in New Zealand!

GIANT INSECTS

Wetas are harmless, despite their awesome size. These ground-dwelling insects were common in New Zealand before humans arrived, but they were easy prey for introduced stoats and rats, because they move slowly and cannot fly. Today, they survive on mammal-free islands, but are rare elsewhere.

ReDiscovery

Once thought to be extinct, the takahé was rediscovered in 1948, on New Zealand's South Island. Today, this flightless bird is carefully protected, and its numbers are slowly going up.

spotlight on kiwis

Although they are still quite common, New Zealand's most famous birds – kiwis – are becoming endangered by predatory mammals. Stoats on the North Island kill more than 15,000 brown kiwi chicks every year.

FACE OF A KILLER

The stoat is one of the worst enemies of New Zealand's native animals. A small but fierce hunter, it kills takahés and kiwis, and also feeds on their eggs. Stoats were brought to New Zealand to control rabbits, but they soon ran out of control. Today, only offshore islands are stoat-free.

Mammals at war

MAMMALS CAN LOOK CUTE and cuddly, but when they run wild far from home, they can have a lethal effect on local wildlife. Mink, cats and foxes can wipe out their defenceless prey, while squirrels and rabbits grab so much food that they make it hard for other animals to survive.

MINK VERSUS MINK

American mink were brought to Europe more than a century ago to be farmed for their fur, but some escaped. Cunning and skilful hunters, they are a menace to fish, small mammals and water birds. Ironically, they have helped make the European mink extinct.

Spotlight on mini-marsupials

In Australia, kangaroos are thriving, but many small marsupials are in deep trouble. They are easy prey for cats and foxes, and some kinds have been completely wiped out.

ReDiscovery

In 1961, Leadbeater's possum was rediscovered in Australia after being "extinct" for more than 50 years. Like many small marsupials, it comes out at night, and it feeds high up in trees. It is still critically endangered, and at risk from forest fires.

SQUIRREL VERSUS SQUIRREL

You are unlikely to spot a red squirrel in England. That's because red squirrels have been driven out by grey ones, which originally came from North America. Grey squirrels are bigger and more aggressive than red ones, and wherever they move in, red squirrels soon disappear.

500 million RABBITS threaten Australia's native wildlife.

AUSTRALIA'S RABBIT PLAGUE

Rabbits were taken to Australia by Europeans more than 150 years ago. Although fewer than 50 were released, their numbers soon exploded into millions, creating a rabbit plague. Today, the rabbit is Australia's number one farmland pest, and its massive appetite makes it a major threat to Australia's native plant-eating mammals.

BACK from the brink

In Western Australia, a giant nature reserve has been created to protect native marsupials. Covering more than 1,000 square kilometres, it is sealed off by high-security fencing, and by a 'no man's land' containing poisoned bait.

Underwater invaders

ALL OVER THE WORLD, FRESHWATER wildlife is threatened by alien invaders. Some of these water animals arrive by accident, but many have been released deliberately – for fishing, or for food. Once the invaders have moved in, it's almost impossible to move them out.

spotlight on Waterweeds...
Some of the world's worst weeds are plants that float on fresh water. Water hyacinth, from South America, can grow so quickly when introduced elsewhere that it clogs up lakes and shades out water wildlife.

AFRICA'S VANISHING FISH
This beautiful fish is a cichlid – one of hundreds of kinds that live in Africa's Rift Valley lakes. Rift Valley cichlids have highly specialized lifestyles, which mean that they are easily harmed by underwater invaders.

CLAWED KILLER
The signal crayfish, from North America, was brought to Europe about 50 years ago. It's good to eat, but it spreads a disease called crayfish plague. It is immune to the disease, but European crayfish are not. As a result, they are quickly dying out.

DEATH FROM THE NILE

The Nile perch is one of Africa's biggest freshwater fish, measuring up to 2m long. In the 1950s, it was introduced into Lake Victoria. The lake originally had more than 500 different kinds of freshwater fish – that's almost eight times as many as there are in the whole of Europe. But thanks to the Nile perch, half of them have now disappeared.

The Nile perch is an AGGRESSIVE alien with a GIANT appetite.

MUSSEL POWER

Originally from Russia, zebra mussels reached America's Great Lakes in the 1980s, probably by sticking to the hulls of ships. Since then, they have run wild. The little mussels fasten themselves to anything solid, and are so numerous that they can completely clog water pipes and even sink small boats.

PACKING A PUNCH

England's River Thames might seem a strange place to find a Chinese crab. But in recent years, the Chinese mitten crab has invaded Britain's rivers, as well as others in Europe and North America. It burrows its way into riverbanks, endangering other animals that normally live there. It gets its name from the tufts of dark hair on its claws.

Watery Graves

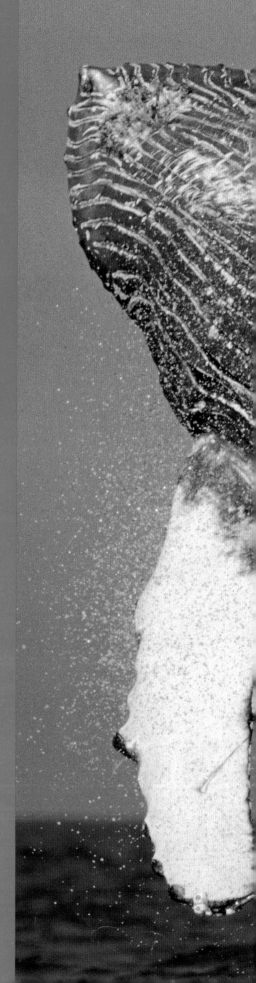

THE OCEANS COVER NEARLY THREE-QUARTERS of the Earth, and in many places they are more than 5km deep. With so much water to hide in, it's hard to imagine any sea animal being threatened, let alone hunted to extinction. But that is exactly what has happened to many species over the last 250 years. Thanks to improvements in technology, humans have become more and more skilled at tracking down and catching sea animals, whether they are fish, seals or whales. Today, many of the world's biggest whales are in danger, and even fish that were once common are becoming scarce. At sea, just as on land, the menace of extinction is growing every year.

Bursting up through the surface, an adult humpback whale shows off its grooved throat and its amazingly long front flippers. Like all great whales, humpbacks have suffered from hunting.

Whales and whaling

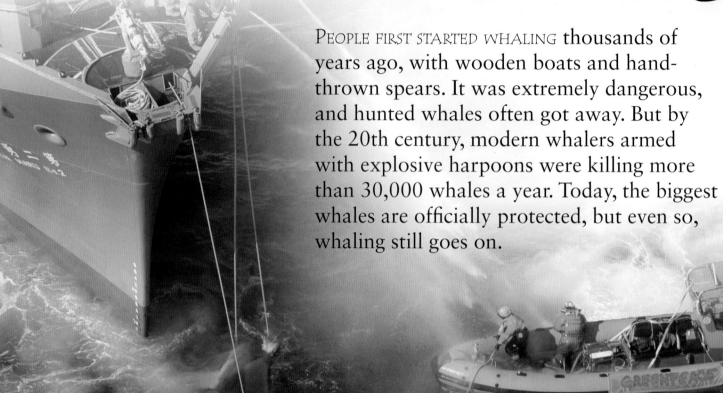

PEOPLE FIRST STARTED WHALING thousands of years ago, with wooden boats and hand-thrown spears. It was extremely dangerous, and hunted whales often got away. But by the 20th century, modern whalers armed with explosive harpoons were killing more than 30,000 whales a year. Today, the biggest whales are officially protected, but even so, whaling still goes on.

CULTURE CLASH

These anti-whaling activists are trying to stop a ship catching minke whales. Most countries have agreed to stop whaling, but some catch hundreds of minke whales every year. Whaling countries say this catch provides important scientific data, but most conservationists believe the hunt is just an excuse to catch whales for their meat.

WHALE-WATCHERS

Getting close to a whale is an unforgettable experience, and it's one that more and more people try every year. These whale-watchers are getting a close-up view of a humpback whale, off the east coast of the USA. Whale-watching is a good way of helping to conserve these amazing creatures. The money spent on it supports local businesses, which enables everyone to benefit from the whaling ban.

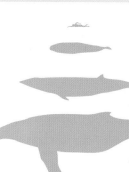

man

Beluga whale

Minke whale

Humpback whale

Blue whale

WHALES BIG AND SMALL

Some whales are less than 5m long. The largest, the blue whale, can be more than 25m long and weigh more than 100 tonnes, but less than 10,000 of these whales are left.

EARLY VICTIMS

Lazing in the chilly waters of the Arctic, these white whales or belugas stand out against the dark blue sea. They are some of the smallest whales, and also some of the first to be hunted for their meat. Because they often come close inshore, they were easy for early whalers to reach in open boats.

STOPPING THE HUNT

Since 1946, whaling has been controlled by the International Whaling Commission (IWC). In 1986, IWC countries decided to launch a temporary halt to whaling, to give endangered species a chance to recover. Every few years the ban is reviewed and members vote on whether to continue it. Most conservationists are fiercely in support of banning whaling.

BACK FROM THE *brink*

The grey whale is one of the few big success stories in whale conservation. Every year the whales migrate between the Arctic and the coast of northern Mexico, where they breed. Hunted almost to extinction, they were given protection in 1946, when the International Whaling Commission (IWC) was formed. There are now about 25,000 grey whales in the eastern Pacific.

Dolphins in danger

IF YOU THINK ABOUT DOLPHINS, you will almost certainly imagine them at sea. But not all the world's dolphins live in saltwater. In South America and Asia, rare freshwater dolphins live in big rivers, where they catch fish with their beak-like jaws. Hemmed in by dams and affected by pollution, these unique river mammals include some of the world's most endangered animals.

FISHING BY SOUND

The boto has pinkish skin, tiny eyes and is almost totally blind. It finds its food by producing high-pitched bursts of sound, which echoes off nearby fish, letting the boto home in on its prey. This system, known as echolocation, is used by all dolphins.

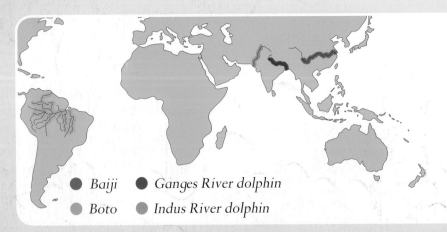

RIVER DOLPHINS OF THE WORLD

South America is home to the largest river dolphin, called the boto. It lives throughout the Amazon and Orinoco river systems, and is the least endangered species, with a total population of more than 10,000. South Asia has two species – the Indus River dolphin and the Ganges River dolphin. They look very similar, and both are officially classified as endangered.

● Baiji   ● Ganges River dolphin
● Boto   ● Indus River dolphin

Dolphins, whales and porpoises are close relatives, and belong to the same group of mammals. Worldwide, nine kinds are seriously endangered, including the tiny vaquita, a porpoise from the Sea of Cortez off western Mexico.

CLOSE ENCOUNTER
This Indus River dolphin is unusually tame, allowing itself to be held and stroked. As a rule, river dolphins are shy, and not nearly as boisterous as dolphins that live at sea. They swim slowly and gently, and can be remarkably tricky to spot, which makes it difficult to gauge how many still survive.

... GOING, going, GONE!

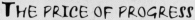

THE END OF THE BAIJI
The baiji survived into the 21st century – but only just. The last confirmed sighting was in 2004, and in 2006, a special expedition was launched to survey the Yangtze River. Scientists spent several weeks searching the surface and listening with underwater microphones. They drew a complete blank, making it almost certain that the baiji is no more.

THE PRICE OF PROGRESS
Towering high over the Yangtze River, these cranes are putting the finishing touches to China's Three Gorges Dam. Dams make life difficult for river dolphins, and they were one of the factors that made the baiji extinct. They split dolphins into small groups, which reduce their chances of finding suitable mates and managing to breed. Apart from dams, the surviving species of river dolphin face other problems, including pollution, and noise from ship's propellers. This interferes with their echolocation, making it harder for them to find food.

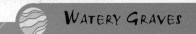
Caught by mistake

WHEN FISHING BOATS HAUL in their catch, fish aren't the only animals that slide out on deck. All kinds of marine life risk being caught as well. Dolphins and turtles get trapped in fishing nets, while albatrosses are hooked by long-line bait that is used far out at sea. Fish is an important human food, but modern fishing methods cause millions of accidental deaths each year.

IN A FLAP

Wandering albatrosses are some of the world's biggest flying birds. They soar in the icy Southern Ocean, and feed by grabbing jellyfish and squid as they glide close to the waves. Unfortunately, they also snatch fishing bait. Once the bird has been hooked, it soon drowns.

FEEDING FRENZY

Black-browed albatrosses often follow fishing boats, swooping on waste that is thrown overboard. They were once common birds, but numbers have plunged in recent years. There are 21 albatross species, but today, fishing threatens 19 of them with extinction.

DEAD ON ARRIVAL

Dolphins feed on fish, which they find by using high-pitched bursts of sound. They are experts at pinpointing their food, but they are not nearly so good at detecting fishing nets. Because dolphins are mammals, they have to surface to breathe. If a dolphin gets stuck in a net, it will die within 20 minutes, unless the net is hauled aboard.

NO HIDING PLACE

These flatfish have been caught by a trawler – a boat that tows a weighted net over the seabed. Trawling nets can be huge, and they pull up all kinds of animals, including starfish, sponges and even corals. In some fishing grounds, the seabed is criss-crossed with deep gouges, showing where trawlers have been at work.

GREAT ESCAPE

How can fishermen prevent turtles drowning in their trawler nets? One way is to fit a specially designed escape hatch. If a turtle enters the net, it is steered upwards by a slanting metal grid. The turtle's weight then pushes open a flap in the net, which allows it to swim away.

Endangered sharks

SHARKS HAVE A DEADLY REPUTATION, and they include some of the most powerful hunters in the sea, but they themselves face an even bigger danger: us. Every year, people kill hundreds of thousands of sharks for food, or simply for fun. Some of the biggest species – including the famous great white – are disappearing fast.

GIANT JAWS

Weighing up to 2 tonnes, this legendary hunter has hundreds of teeth, and a bite nearly 1m wide. The great white shark is the world's biggest predatory fish, but even this cannot ensure its safety. Highly prized by trophy fishermen, it is now in serious danger of dying out.

The world's BIGGEST sharks are *completely* harmless.

UNTIMELY END

This young whale shark, hanging from a crane, is even bigger than a great white. Whale sharks are the world's largest fish, but because they swim slowly, they are easy to catch. They have tiny teeth and their jaws are too weak to bite. Instead, just like many whales, they feed by straining tiny animals out of the water.

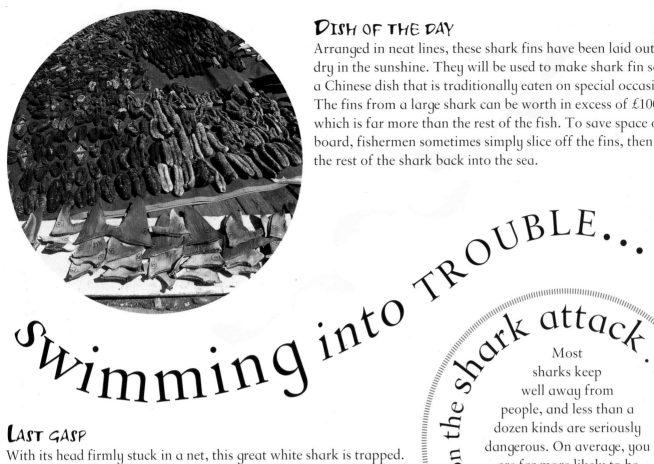

DISH OF THE DAY

Arranged in neat lines, these shark fins have been laid out to dry in the sunshine. They will be used to make shark fin soup, a Chinese dish that is traditionally eaten on special occasions. The fins from a large shark can be worth in excess of £100, which is far more than the rest of the fish. To save space on board, fishermen sometimes simply slice off the fins, then throw the rest of the shark back into the sea.

Swimming into TROUBLE...

LAST GASP

With its head firmly stuck in a net, this great white shark is trapped. It cannot even bite its way to freedom. Huge numbers of sharks end their lives like this – the number has tripled in the last 50 years. Unlike most fish, open-water sharks have to keep swimming in order to get enough oxygen, so they suffocate once they are caught.

spotlight on the shark attack

Most sharks keep well away from people, and less than a dozen kinds are seriously dangerous. On average, you are far more likely to be struck by lightning than to be attacked by a shark.

Pollution and Disease

No one likes being on the receiving end of other people's rubbish, and none of us enjoys being ill. That's why we spend a lot of time and money on creating a healthy environment for ourselves. However, all too often, we don't take nearly as much care of the natural world. Every year, millions of tonnes of plastic are thrown away, and hundreds of artificial chemicals find their way into water, into the air or into the soil beneath our feet. A lot of this pollution is hidden away, but it can have disastrous effects on wildlife.

Plastic can be deadly to wild animals, because it does not break down after it has been thrown away. This herring gull has become entangled with the plastic carrier from a six-pack of cans. Without help, its chances of survival are slim.

Amphibian alert

SOMETHING STRANGE HAS BEEN happening to the world's amphibians: they have started to disappear. Frogs and toads were the first to be affected, but newts and salamanders are now vanishing as well. To begin with, scientists were baffled. They now think that amphibians are being hit by several disasters at once, including pollution, disease and habitat change.

JUNGLE JEWEL
This beautifully coloured frog lives in just one place – a small area of rainforest in Suriname, in South America. Fortunately, the forest is protected, so this frog is safe. Many other amphibians are not so lucky.

NEARLY ONE IN TEN of the world's *amphibians is critically* endangered

ENDANGERED GIANT
The Chinese giant salamander may not be beautiful, but it has one claim to fame: measuring up to 1m long, it's the biggest amphibian in the world. It lives in rivers in central China, but it is critically endangered and struggling to survive. Like many other amphibians, it has been harmed by water pollution, but one of the biggest threats that it faces is being caught and cooked.

BACK FROM THE *brink*

Small things can help amphibians in their fight to survive. This road sign is put up every spring, in places where common toads often cross the road, to alert motorists. Like many frogs, common toads gather in ponds to breed, and many of them have to cross roads on their way.

END OF AN ERA

This picture could not be taken today. That's because golden toads, from Costa Rica, are now extinct. At one time, they used to gather on the forest floor to breed, where, because they were so colourful, they were often photographed. The last time they bred was in 1987, and the last survivor – a male – was seen in 1989. The golden toad's disappearance made the headlines worldwide.

HOLDING TIGHT

It takes a firm grip to keep hold of a goliath frog. Found in rivers in West Africa, this heavyweight amphibian can weigh as much as a large chicken, and it measures up to 80cm with its legs stretched out. Like the Chinese giant salamander, it faces lots of problems, including pollution, habitat change and, most of all, being caught for food.

Accidental deaths

DURING THE 1950s, many birds of prey were poisoned by a powerful new insecticide called DDT. America's national bird, the bald eagle, came close to extinction before DDT was banned. But despite this brush with disaster, the problem of accidental poisoning has still not gone away. Every year, millions of animals become the victims of chemicals that find their way into the wild.

TROUBLE AT THE TOP

Birds of prey, such as the bald eagle, are particularly at risk to poisons. This is because a predator's body stores up chemicals that are in its prey. DDT affected bald eagles by making them lay eggs with thin shells. When they sat on their eggs, the shells cracked, so they were unable to hatch any young.

ATTACK FROM THE AIR

Swooping low over a field, this plane is spraying a crop with a pesticide. In many parts of the world, farmers rely on chemicals like these to keep plant-eating animals under control. However, as well as killing pests, farmland chemicals often endanger other kinds of wildlife, including animals that feed on the pests themselves. Pesticides also have a habit of spreading – in water, in the air and in food.

Man-made chemicals can last for years once they find their way into the wild. Poisonous ones have been discovered in animals all over the world, including turtles, whales, penguins and polar bears.

NATURAL ALLIES

This lacewing is feeding on aphids – small sap-sucking insects that are some of the worst farmland pests. On many farms, predators such as lacewings are often killed by pesticides, but these helpful animals can be specially bred and released in fields, cutting down on the amount of chemicals that have to be used.

POISONOUS chemicals can **build up** *when one kind of animal* EATS ANOTHER.

BELLY UP

Many man-made chemicals can cause havoc if they get into lakes and rivers. Fish absorb them through their gills, or in their food. Dead fish are often the first sign of a bad pollution incident.

SCENTED TRAPS

One way to get rid of pests is to trap them with their own scent. The chemicals in these scents are called pheromones, and insects use them to find each other when they breed. Each kind of insect has different ones. When they are produced artificially, these pheromones can be used to trap pests, but nothing else. Insects are amazingly good at smelling these airborne chemicals – some can sniff them out more than two kilometres downwind.

Oil spills

WE ALL NEED OIL. Even if you don't travel by car, oil is used to produce all kinds of things that you use, from plastic bags to mobile phones. Every year, millions of tonnes of oil are delivered by giant tankers, and with so much oil on board, even the smallest accidents can produce major leaks. A full-blown disaster, such as a collision or a fire, can cause pollution that harms wildlife for years.

BLACK OUT
Rare jackass penguins, from South Africa, live and breed close to one of the world's busiest shipping routes. In the last 30 years, they have been badly affected by oil spills. Normally black with a white chest and face, this penguin has been completely blackened by oil.

EMERGENCY AT SEA
Its deck ablaze, this stricken tanker is leaking oil into the sea. Oil is lighter than water, so it floats on the surface – the worst possible place for it to be for many sea animals. Birds get coated with oil when they swim or dive, and seals sometimes swallow it when they come up to breathe.

THE OIL in a *big tanker* could fill *125* olympic-sized swimming pools.

BATH TIME

Oil sticks to birds' feathers, and slowly hardens as time goes by. The only way to get it off is to gently brush it away with detergent. Here a bird is being de-oiled before being released back into the wild.

SEA OTTER WITH BABY

When a tanker ran aground in Alaska in 1989, it created one of the biggest oil spills on record. Among the victims were 5,000 sea otters. These animals groom their fur by licking it clean. In Alaska, the sea otters were slowly poisoned as they tried to lick the oil away.

CLEANING UP

When oil reaches the shore, the only way to get rid of it is to pick it up, or bulldoze it away. A much better tactic is to stop it spreading in the first place. If a tanker starts to leak, the oil can sometimes be kept in place by floating booms. Detergent is then sprayed on the oil to break it up.

Disease on the move

IF YOU CATCH A COLD, your body will fight off the infection, and the cold will go away. Wild animals also catch diseases, most of which do little lasting harm. But when humans and wild animals mix, much more dangerous diseases occasionally get a chance to spread. They can flare up without warning, sometimes bringing threatened species to the very edge of extinction.

DANGER IN THE AIR

Mosquitoes are dangerous animals because they often carry disease. They spread malaria in humans and also in wild animals. There are several types of malaria, apart from the one that humans catch. For example, one kind attacks chimps, while another, called avian malaria, targets birds. Mosquitoes lay their eggs in water, so anything that collects rain – from old bottles to tyres – can help malaria to spread.

ON THE RETREAT

The 'i'iwi, from the Hawaiian Islands, is fighting a battle against avian malaria. The disease was introduced when humans arrived, bringing mosquitoes with them. At one time, 'I'iwis lived in forests all over the islands. Today, they have disappeared from low ground, as this is inhabited by the mosquitoes.

big trouble from a tiny BITE

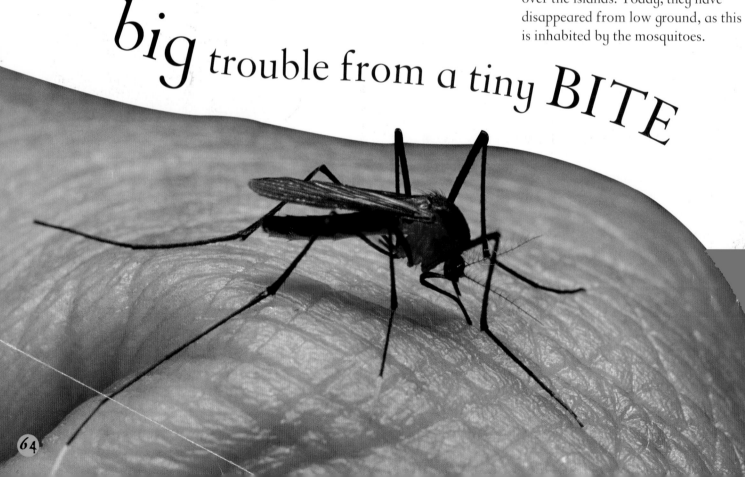

SHRINKING PACK

With their big ears and blotchy fur, African wild dogs are only distant relatives of the dogs we keep as pets. However, they can catch the same diseases. Two of these – rabies and distemper – have helped to wipe out wild dogs in 25 African countries.

BACK FROM THE *brink*

The Mediterranean monk seal is one of the world's rarest sea mammals. It is critically endangered, with only about 500 left alive. In 1997, a mysterious epidemic almost wiped them out. Fortunately, enough seals survived to head off the threat of extinction. Scientists are still not sure what caused the disease.

OUT OF THE FOREST

Gorillas and humans can both catch Ebola fever – a deadly disease from Africa first identified in the 1970s. Hundreds of people have died of the disease, and so have up to 5,000 lowland gorillas, which live in Central and West Africa. Gorillas are already in danger from hunting and deforestation, so the disease could not have come at a worse time.

Global warming

DURING THE NEXT 50 YEARS, global warming looks set to make dramatic changes to our planet. Already, summer temperatures have reached record levels in some parts of the world, and farmers have been hit by long-running droughts. The Arctic's sea ice is shrinking, and many mountain glaciers are melting fast. It's not the first time the Earth's climate has changed, but it is the first time that humans have been partly to blame. At present, no one knows exactly how wild animals will fare, but the early signs are not good.

FUTURE ON ICE

The polar bear has become an emblem of global warming because it depends on sea ice to survive. Polar bears don't eat much in the summer, but in the winter, they wander far over the frozen sea to catch seals. The less winter ice there is, the harder it is for them to reach their food.

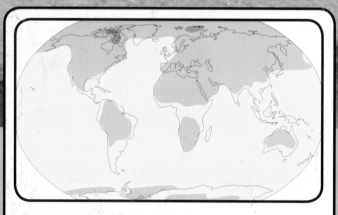

MIXED FORTUNES

This map shows how much warmer the world may be by the end of this century. In the dark-red areas, the average temperature could rise by more than 3°C. This may not sound much, but it could have a huge effect on plants, animals and other living things.

POLAR BEARS could become *extinct* by the end of *this* century.

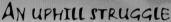

UPS AND DOWNS

Adélie penguins love a crowd. They breed in gigantic groups on rocky coasts, and feed on tiny sea animals called krill. Today, krill is common, but as the seas warm up, it may become harder to find. Penguins won't be the only animals to lose out, because krill is an important food for many seals and whales as well.

THREATENED REEFS

Global warming is already harming the world's coral reefs. It causes stormy weather, which stirs up the water, making it harder for corals to grow. More importantly, it causes coral bleaching (see page 35), which can kill whole reefs in just a few weeks.

AN UPHILL STRUGGLE

Apollo butterflies live high up on mountains, and they keep warm by basking in the sunshine. But in the years to come, they could find themselves in the shade, because trees will be able to grow further up on mountainsides. To survive, the butterflies will have to move higher still, or they will face dying out.

TURBULENT TIMES

In East Africa, wildebeest have to cross big rivers as they migrate across the grassy plains. In recent years, storms have filled the rivers to bursting point, and lots of wildebeest have been swept away in the floods. Many scientists think that global warming has helped to trigger the unusually heavy rain.

67

...What Next?

NO ONE CAN PREDICT WHAT the world will be like 25 years from now, and it's even harder to guess how the planet will look in 50 or 100 years' time. But one thing is certain: there will be more people, and less room for the world's wildlife. Humans already take more than their share of the Earth's resources and in the future we will use up even more. Endangered animals will need even better protection, because once a species has become extinct, nothing can bring it back.

Giant pandas are the world's favourite animals – that's why so much effort has been spent helping them to survive. But conservation means protecting all animals, whether or not they look good.

Captive breeding

THE BEST WAY TO SAVE ANIMALS is to protect the habitats where they live. But if a species is in extreme danger, emergency action is needed to stop it dying out. The surviving animals are sometimes caught, and then encouraged to breed in special reserves or zoos. If all goes well, their numbers steadily increase, until some of them can be released back into the wild.

STAR APPEAL

The giant panda is the world's most famous endangered animal. It lives in the mountain forests of central China, where its thick black-and-white coat protects it from the winter cold. But pandas face many problems, including forest clearance and illegal hunting. Without captive breeding, this fascinating animal might have disappeared from the wild.

BOUNCING BABIES

For many years, Chinese scientists tried to persuade captive pandas to breed. But until recently, very few adult pandas became parents. In the last ten years, a lot has been learned about the behaviour of these animals, and the breeding programme has been much more successful. These cuddly panda cubs were all born in captivity, at China's Wolong Nature Reserve.

Some animals survive in captivity even though they have become extinct in the wild. One of them is Spix's macaw, a large grey-blue parrot from Brazil. Unlike most parrots, it is a very fussy eater, feeding on fruit from just one kind of tree.

BACK FROM THE *brink*

The California condor is the biggest bird in North America. By 1987, there were only 22 left in the wild, so the decision was taken to catch them all, using dead animals as bait. Thanks to the breeding programme, the condor is now in better shape. There are about 150 birds in the wild, and the same number in zoos.

READY TO RUN

With its long legs and red fur, the maned wolf, from South America, is rarer than the grey wolf, and also much harder to find. It lives in grassland and woodland – habitats that are often fenced off and turned into fields. Its numbers have been falling for years, but it is now being successfully bred in zoos.

HELPING HAND

Turtles hatch from eggs and then scuttle towards the sea. But predators often dig up turtle eggs, or catch young turtles as they race across the sand. Captive breeding gives them a much better chance, by making sure that the eggs and young are safe.

Saving habitats

THERE IS NO POINT RESCUING animals if there is nowhere left for them to live in the wild. That's why saving natural habitats is just as important as protecting animals themselves. A habitat gives animals everything they need, including space, shelter and the right kind of food. Protecting habitats might sound easy, but there is much more to it than sitting back and letting nature do the work.

THIS WON'T HURT

Taking aim from a helicopter, a wildlife ranger shoots an elephant with a tranquillizer dart. It's one way of dealing with a difficult problem: too many elephants and too little space. Once the elephant is unconscious, it will be taken away by truck to another wildlife reserve where there is more room.

ORPHANED ORANGS

These cute young orang-utans face a barrowful of problems. Their natural habitat, Indonesia's tropical rainforest, is disappearing at a record rate as its trees are cut down for their timber. To save the orang-utan, the remaining forest must be saved as well. Unless this happens, these youngsters will spend their lives in zoos.

THE RIGHT TO ROAM

Big predators, such as this jaguar, need lots of space to move about in, and that can be difficult to find in today's crowded world. One way around the problem is to create special wildlife corridors. These are pieces of natural habitat that link different nature reserves – like corridors connecting different rooms. Animals can use these corridors to roam, without humans getting in their way.

HEAD IN THE CLOUDS

Many animals need a special kind of habitat to survive. The quetzal is one of them. This beautiful bird lives in cloud-covered forests in Central America's mountains – no other kind of habitat will do. Quetzals rarely survive long in captivity, so saving the quetzal means saving the cloud forest as well.

Making WILDLIFE pay

spotlight on the national parks

The world's biggest national park isn't in Africa, but far away in northeast Greenland. It covers nearly 100,000 square kilometres – that's almost as big as the whole of England.

TOURISTS TO THE RESCUE

These tourists are getting a bird's-eye view of this Samoan rainforest – one of many exciting ways of exploring the natural world. This kind of travel, called ecotourism, is a fast-growing business, and it can play a big part in saving habitats, by making them pay their way. To work, ecotourism has to earn money for local people. This gives them a good reason for protecting habitats instead of harming them.

73

Looking ahead

Today, there is no shortage of bad news about the world's wildlife. Every year, more animals become endangered, and dozens of species become extinct. However, there is some good news as well. People have become much more concerned about endangered species, and scientists are finding new ways to help animals in trouble.

MANY *animals* will need PROTECTION to survive.

UNCERTAIN FUTURE
Ignoring the people behind it, this tiger seems to have more important things on its mind. The future will be difficult for all tigers, as they face the twin threats of hunting and habitat change. They will survive in safari parks and zoos, but maybe not in the wild.

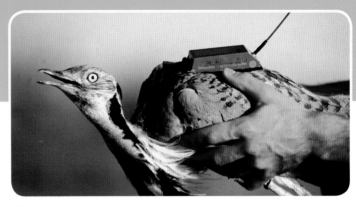

OUTSIDE BROADCAST

With a radio transmitter strapped to its back, this bustard is easy for scientists to track. Hi-tech gadgets already play a big part in conservation. In the future, they are likely to be smaller, smarter and even more useful.

FOLLOW THE LEADER

Sixty years after it was first given protection, the grey whale is flourishing again. In the future, other whales could follow its lead. An international agreement protects most of them from hunting, and two special whale sanctuaries have been set up, one in the Indian Ocean, the other in the Southern Ocean around Antarctica.

Discoveries

Every year, hundreds of new species are discovered and identified by scientists who are working in remote parts of the world. Most of them are insects and other small land animals, or worms and other soft-bodied creatures that live in freshwater or the sea. But just occasionally, new mammals are found. Since the year 2000, these new discoveries have included two species of whale, a pygmy sloth from Panama and an amazing 30 kinds of bat.

SOARAWAY SUCCESS

Forty years ago, the red kite was one of Britain's rarest birds. But in 1989, six kites were brought from Sweden and released into the wild. It was the start of a spectacular recovery for this sharp-eyed hunter, which soars high up over woods and fields. Today, Britain has at least 2,000 red kites, and the number is still growing.

Glossary

Alien species An animal or a plant that has escaped into the wild after being brought in from far away.

Amphibian A frog, toad, salamander or newt. Amphibians are animals that spend part of their lives in water and part on land.

Bird of prey A bird that hunts other animals, catching them with its sharp claws. Apart from owls, birds of prey all hunt by day.

Camouflage Colours and patterns that help an animal to hide. Most camouflaged animals blend in with their surroundings and so are difficult to spot unless they move.

Captive breeding A way of helping endangered species by keeping them in captivity and encouraging them to breed. In captivity, the young are safe from predators, so their numbers often increase faster than they would in the wild.

Conservation Anything that helps to stop animals, or the habitats in which they live, disappearing. Conservation organisations, such as Greenpeace, work hard to limit the damage that humans do to the natural world.

Coral bleaching An illness triggered by unusually warm water that makes corals turn white. Corals sometimes recover from bleaching, but if the water temperature stays high, they die.

Critically endangered Facing a very high risk of dying out in the wild.

Deforestation Cutting down forests for their timber or to open up land for farming. Deforestation has been happening for thousands of years, but since the 1970s, it has been particularly severe in the tropics, where most of the world's rainforests grow.

Distemper A disease that infects dogs and their wild relatives. Distemper is a problem for some endangered species because they can catch it from dogs.

Domestic animal An animal that lives under human control rather than in the wild. Domestic animals include pets and also animals that are raised on farms.

Echolocation A way of finding food that is used by dolphins, bats and some other animals. They make high-pitched bursts of sound and then listen for the echoes that come back from nearby objects.

Ecotourism Going on holiday to see wild places and wildlife. Ecotourists visit all kinds of different places, from rainforests to Antarctica.

Endangered Facing a high risk of becoming extinct in the wild.

Evolve When living things evolve, they slowly change, so that they become better at their way of life. Evolution does not happen in a single lifetime. Instead, the changes build up over many generations, each time living things breed.

Extinct No longer existing anywhere on Earth. Some animals are extinct in the wild, but still survive in zoos.

Fossil Prehistoric remains that have turned to stone after being buried in the ground. Fossils enable scientists to study animals that became extinct a long time ago.

Gills Special flaps that fish use to get oxygen from the water around them.

Habitat The kind of surroundings that living things need to survive. There are many different habitats on Earth, from deserts and mountains to forests and freshwater wetlands. Unlike humans, most animals can live in only one habitat.

Habitat change Altering natural habitats in ways that harm the wildlife that lives in them.

Horn In most animals, a horn is a hollow spike. In rhinos, horns are solid, and made of the same substance that they have in their hair and hooves.

Insecticide A chemical that is designed to kill insects. Some insecticides come from plants, but most are man-made.

Introduced animal Any kind of animal that has been taken from its natural home, and released somewhere else, often far away.

Ivory The hard creamy white substance that makes up an elephant's tusks. Some whales also have ivory in their teeth.

Krill Small, shrimp-like animals that live in the Southern Ocean. Krill live in huge shoals, or swarms, which can weigh more than a billion tonnes.

Long-line fishing A way of fishing that uses thousands of baited hooks, trailing from a long line in the sea.

Malaria A blood disease that attacks humans, and also many wild mammals and birds. It is spread by mosquitoes.

Marsupial A mammal that raises its young in a pouch. Most of the world's marsupials live in Australia, but some are found in North and South America.

Microbe A living thing that is visible only with a microscope. Almost all animals contain microbes, and some depend on them to survive.

Migrate Carrying out long journeys at particular times of the year. Many animals migrate to the far north to breed. In the autumn, they migrate south to escape the cold of winter.

Mollusc A soft-bodied animal that is usually protected by a hard shell. Snails and mussels are molluscs.

Native species An animal or a plant in its natural home. Native species can be very common if their home is left undisturbed, but they often have few defences against outsiders. If predators are introduced, native species can quickly become extinct.

Persecuted Deliberately killed or harmed.

Pesticide A man-made chemical that is designed to kill pests.

Poaching Illegal hunting.

Pollution Damaging living things by releasing harmful substances in the wild. Pollution can be caused by many different things, from household rubbish to the invisible gases in car exhausts.

Predator Any animal that gets its food by killing and eating other animals. Most predators catch other animals one by one, but some, including big whales, catch thousands of animals at a time.

Primate A mammal that has forward-pointing eyes, long arms, and fingers that grip. Humans are primates, and so are apes, monkeys, lemurs and aye-ayes.

Rabies A dangerous disease that affects some mammals, including bats, dogs, foxes, and also humans. Animals often catch rabies by being bitten by an animal that already has the disease.

Range The part of the world where an animal species lives. Some species have big ranges, but others have ranges just a few kilometres wide.

Reintroduced animal An animal that has been released back into an area where it once lived, but where it then died out.

Species A group of living things that look the same, and that breed together in the wild. So far, scientists have found two million different species on Earth. About half of them are animals; the rest include plants, fungi, bacteria and other kinds of microscopic life.

Tropical forest Forest that grows in warm parts of the world. There is no winter in the tropics, so tropical trees can often grow all year round.

Tusk An extra-long tooth that often looks like a horn.

Vulnerable At risk from extinction, either now or in the near future.

Wetland A freshwater habitat. Wetlands include rivers, lakes, marshes and swamps.

Index

Acknowledgements

The publishers would like to thank the following for permission to use their material. Every care has been taken to trace copyright holders. However, if there have been unintentional omissions or failure to trace copyright holders, we apologise, and will, if informed, endeavour to make corrections in any future edition.

KEY
t = top; c = centre; b = bottom; r = right; l = left; m = middle

Ardea 29tr (John Daniels); 29b (Pat Morris); 31tl (John Cancalosi); 31b (Jean-Paul Ferrero); 32t (Keith & Liz Laidler); 36–7 (Jean-Paul Ferrero); 43c (Jean-Paul Ferrero); 44b (John Clegg); 50 (Pat Morris); 51cr (Keith & Liz Laidler); 55b (Valerie Taylor); 60tl (Tom & Pat Leeson); 67b (Yann Arthus-Bertrand); 70t (Adrian Warren)

Associated Press 21tr (Itsuo Inouye)

Auscape 40b (John Shaw); 41c (Mike Langford)

Corbis 10 background (Gianni Dagli Orti); 10bl (Bettmann); 11mr (Raymond Gehman); 11br (DK Limited); 14t (Layne Kennedy); 16tr (Bettmann); 20t (John Conrad); 26–7 (Paulo Fridman); 68–9 (Xiao Wang/epa)

Cosmographics 50bl; 66bl

FLPA 2–3 (David Hosking); 16bl (Frits Van Daalen/Foto Natura); 17bl (Terry Whittaker); 28b (Konrad Wothe/Minden Pictures); 29tl (Fritz Polking); 30b (Hugh Clark); 33t (Panda Photo); 34b (Reinhard Dirscher); 35tl (Fred Bavendam/Minden Pictures); 35b (Norbert Wu/Minden Pictures); 38t (Frans Lanting); 38b (Colin Marshall); 39b (Tui de Roy); 42t (Tim Fitzharris/Minden Pictures); 42b (Rod Williams); 44c (Foto Natura Stock); 45c (Wil Meinderts/Foto Natura); 48b (Flip Nicklin/Minden Pictures); 53r (S. Jonasson); 54l (Fred Bavendam/Minden Pictures);

58t (Michael & Patricia Fogden); 59tl (Michael & Patricia Fogden/Minden Pictures); 60br (Gordon Roberts); 63c (Frans Lanting); 66 (David Hosking); 67c (Fred Bavendam/Minden Pictures); 71t (Michael Durham/Minden Pictures); 72t (Frans Lanting); 75tl (Konrad Wothe); 75br Mark Sisson

Getty Images 6–7 (Minden Pictures); 10br (Kenneth Garrett); 15bl (ZSSD/Minden Pictures); 20br (Zhinong Xi); 22 (Bill Curtsinger/National Geographic); 23t (Kwai Chow Wong/AFP); 30t (Jim & Jamie Dutcher/National Geographic); 61tl (Roger Bosch/AFP); 63t (Leon Neal); 70b (Liu Jin); 20b (Zhinong Xi)

Glenbow Archives 14bl

Greepeace 48t (Kate Davison); 53tl (Rowlands)

Hedgehoghouse 41t (John Weeber); 41b (Marty Taylor)

Lewa Wildlife Conservancy 19t & b (Richard Moller)

National Library of Medicine 12bl

Nature Picture Library 52cr (Pete Oxford); 55t (Jurgen Freund)

NHPA 15br (Paul Brough); 31tr (Daniel Heuclin); 32b (Simon Booth); 33br (Andy Rouse); 33bl (Joe Blossom); 38c (A.N.T. Photolibrary); 39t (Karl Switak); 43t (Manfred Danegger); 43b (Ann & Steven Toon); 52b (John Shaw); 58b (Daniel Heuclin); 59tr (Roger Tidman); 62l (Martin Harvey); 64b (Haroldo Paolo Jr); 64t (Bill Coster); 65t (Andy Rouse); 67tr (Jordi Bas Casas); 72b (David Higgs); 73c (Kevin Schafer)

PA Photos 27t (AP); 49cr (Koji Sasahara/AP)

Photolibrary.com 1 (TB Photo); 4–5 (Elliot Neep); 12tl (Imagestate Ltd); 15tr (Werner

Bollmann); 17r (Patricio Robles Gil); 18bl (Steve Turner); 19br (Elliot Neep); 21b (Daniel Cox); 26cl (Alan & Sandy Carey); 26b (Mary Plage); 27 b & cr (Animals Animals/Earth Sciences); 28t (JTB Photo); 35cr (Norbert Wu); 45t (Mark Deeble & Victoria Stone/Flat Dog Productions); 46–7 (Ushioda Masa); 49tr (Doug Allan/Tartan Dragon); 49br (Howard Hall); 51br (Panorama Media, Beijing Ltd); 56–7 (Patti Murray); 61r (Bill Beatty); 62r (Danilo Balducci); 71r (OSF/Stan Osolinski); 73r (David Kirkland); 74 (Milse Milse

Photoshot 13tr (R. Sorensen & J. Olsen); 54br (Newscom)

Reuters 51tr (Kim Lee)

Shutterstock 8–9 (EcoPrint); 12 (Verena Ludemann); 13b (Verena Ludemann); 18–19 (Robert Hardholt); 23bl (Joseph M. Penalver Rufas); 34–5 (Speta); 65br (Stepan Jezek)

Still Pictures 23cr (François Gilson); 24–5 (S. Chamnanrith/UNESCO); 45b (F. Hecker); 63b (DAS-Fotoarchiv); 65br (Biosphoto/Marquez Francisco); 67cl (Biosphoto/Beauchene Fabrice); 71b (Kelvin Aitken); 73t (Michael Sewell); 75tr (Michael Gunther)

TopFoto 40t (from Extinct Birds by Errol Fuller

UK Management Authority for CITES 23

WCS John Goodrich and AMUR/amur. org.uk 21t

Jacket image front: NHPA/Kevin Schafer; back: Bill Curtsinger/National Geographic Image Collection; NHPA/Thomas Kitchin & Victoria Hurst;NHPA/Martin Harvey; NHPA/Anthony Bannister.

Useful Websites

Ask an adult to help you find additional websites and check them out before you use them.

ARKive
http://www.arkive.org/
ARKive is a huge online image bank of animals and plants, including ones that are threatened with extinction. Its profiles often include film clips as well as photos, and even the sounds that animals make.

Greenpeace
http://www.greenpeace.org/international/
The world's leading conservation organisation, Greenpeace was founded in 1971. Greenpeace activists tackle all kinds of environmental problems, from whaling to deforestation, and they are often in the headlines.

IUCN Red List
http://www.iucnredlist.org/
The Red List is an online list of all the world's threatened species, with detail of where they live, and what threats they face. The list is constantly updated as scientists find out more about animals in the wild.

World Wide Fund for Nature
http://www.panda.org/
The WWF has been working to protect the environment for nearly 50 years. Today, its scientists and volunteers are at work on more than 2,000 projects in dozens of different countries. You can find out about many of these projects on the WWF website.